How to be a Confident Kid

By Kay Drummond

With help from Samantha

Copyright © 2013 Kay Drummond

and Samantha Drummond

All rights reserved

ISBN: 1482520095

ISBN-13: 978-1482520095

Photos: Dreamstime.com

Dedicated to all children throughout the world.

May each of you come to realise how important and

special you are.

Table of Contents

Chapter 1 Self Belief 1

Chapter 2 Having The Right Attitude.................5

Chapter 3 Hurt Feelings.............................9

Chapter 4 Feeling Scared...........................13

Chapter 5 Being Brave..............................19

Chapter.6 Affirmations.............................23

Chapter 7 Making Friends...........................27

Chapter 8 Facing Up To The Truth...................31

Chapter 9 Trying My Best...........................35

Chapter 10 Feeling Left Out........................39

Chapter 11 Sharing.................................43

Chapter 12 I Can Do it Thoughts....................47

Chapter 13 Being Special...........................51

Chapter 14 Feeling Important.......................55

Believe

in

yourself

You

are

amazing

Chapter 1

Self Belief

Grandma told me when I want to believe in myself, I should start talking to myself! How dumb does that sound! My Gran seems to have weird ideas that make sense once she tells me what she means.

She explained that I am what I tell myself. When I keep saying I can't do things or that I am useless, this is what I believe. I stop myself from doing things because I don't think I can. This must be true, because a lot of the time I don't even try to do something because I have told myself I can't.

Do you feel like this too?

Grandma says these are called negative thoughts, and it is these thoughts that stop me from doing what I would like to.

Help! Growing up isn't easy is it?

Thoughts are important. Grandma has told me that everything I do is because of a thought I have had. She told me I have thousands and thousands of thoughts come into my head every day, and that I only act on the ones that I bring into my mind.

I know I sometimes choose thoughts that make me unhappy, do you? My Grandma has said that when I do this I can't stop thinking about what upsets me, which is a shame, because if I could stop thinking horrible things I would feel better. She said that every time I think about the bad thoughts I bring back the unhappiness. I think Gran's onto something here, because I know the more I think about what made me angry, or sad, the worse I feel!

What about you, do you think Gran might be right?

Happy thoughts make me feel good about myself. Grandma says these are positive thoughts, and positive thoughts are good because they make me feel happy inside.

I agree with this, do you?

She said that positive thoughts give me confidence. This is why Grandma says I should talk to myself!

She said that when I hear a thought come into my mind that says I can't do something, straight away change it to one that tells me I can. I am going to do this the next time I think I can't do something. Why don't you try this as well? We are going to be so confident when we grow up if we do this all the time aren't we? I love it!

Special Note to you

In class today I had to recite a poem. I was so scared, my heart was racing and I felt sick because I thought everyone was looking at me.

Then I remembered what Grandma had told me, and I said,

"Calm down, relax, give it a go." I said to myself "I can do this."

Guess what?

I did it, I did it!

Grandma was right! She was so proud of me when I told her! What she is telling me really works. When I do my best I can succeed. When I really try hard, and trust in myself, I can do things I never thought I could! I hope you try next time too!

Thanks for the advice Grandma

Chapter 2

Having The Right Attitude

When I woke up this morning I felt sad. Do you feel this way sometimes? I don't know why because nothing bad had happened. I thought it was a sign that I was going to have a bad day.

Grandma must have seen I had a sad look on my face because she asked what was wrong. I told her I didn't know, I just felt unhappy.

She told me my attitude was the problem. I asked her what she meant, and she explained that attitude is how I feel about things, the thoughts I am thinking. Grandma told me I can choose how I want to feel. Did I want to feel happy or sad? She said it was up to me what I chose.

She said my thoughts are important, and that only I could have them, which kind of made sense because I am the one inside my mind. She asked why would I want to choose sad thoughts when I could choose happy ones.

I thought about this for a while, and decided there could be something in what she told me.

What do you think?

Sometimes I feel unhappy and don't know why, so I think I could choose happy thoughts if I wanted.

She explained that throughout my life I will have choices to make and that only I can make them. This is good to know because it makes me the ruler of my life. I will be in charge of myself when I grow up, because, as my Gran has said, my thoughts are mine, and no one else can give them to me!

Special Note to you

From now on I am going to change my attitude. I am going to have happy thoughts and feel happy inside.

What about you, do you think it's a good idea to have happy thoughts instead of ones that make you sad? I hope so!

Thanks Grandma

I
AM
BRAVE

Chapter 3

Hurt Feelings

The other day someone said something horrible to me and it made me feel bad. Grandma asked me what was wrong and I told her a boy in my class had said something horrible to me.

She told me it wasn't the words that hurt me. I didn't know what she meant because I knew how I felt, and I felt hurt. She said it was the way I reacted to what the boy said that had made me feel bad. She also said that if I hadn't cared about what he told me I wouldn't have a problem.

I had to think about this for a while because I wasn't sure what she meant, and I know that when my Grandma gives me advice, what she tells me always makes sense.

Then I remembered the time my friend Christopher said I looked like a big fat bumble bee because I was wearing a black and yellow striped top. I laughed at what he said and forgot about it. Had I felt hurt about what he said and kept on thinking about it, I would have felt horrible, but, because I didn't let his words annoy me, I didn't have a problem.

This must be what my Gran means. It was my own thoughts that caused my hurt feelings.

Right! The next time someone says something I don't like, I am going to do my best not to feel hurt. I will think about something that makes me happy, in this way I won't have a problem.

Why not see if you can do this too when someone says something you don't like?

Grandma told me it isn't easy not reacting but to try really hard to forget any nasty words that are spoken to me. She also said that when someone says something I don't like, to walk away from them, and try hard not to speak to them or disagree with what they say. She said some kids are bullies and seem to enjoy being nasty, and it's best not to take any notice of what they say.

Special Note to you

The other day I was walking to school when a girl I didn't know came up, pushed me, said my hair looked horrible, and told me to get out of the way.

I felt scared, and then I remembered to do what my Grandma told me. I turned and walked away and didn't stop to look round! Phew! She didn't come after me, otherwise I would have gone straight into school and told my teacher. I tried hard not to think about what she said, and told myself she was wrong, my hair looked really nice. This helped to stop me feeling unhappy.

Grandma really does know everything

Chapter 4

Feeling Scared

I'm starting a new school and I'm feeling worried because none of my friends are going to the same school as I am.

I need to speak to Grandma!

Grandma explained that a lot of the kids will be as worried as I am and that the best thing for me to do is to be brave. She has said that friendship has to be given, and for me to talk to other kids first.

She suggested that I ask all sorts of questions about themselves. Things like where they live, what their hobbies are, who is their favourite singer, favourite song, how many in their family, do they have a dog or another pet?

Grandma said that when the person answers my question it gives me something to say back to them, and in this way we have more to talk about, and can become friends.

She has even said that it's important to be a good listener because some people like to be listened to, so I must remember that if I want people to listen to me I must be prepared to listen to them first.

Special Note to you

I did feel quite scared when I went into school. There were lots of kids talking in groups and I didn't know anyone. I just stood there feeling horrible, lonely, and sort of embarrassed.

I hated feeling like this so decided to test my Grandma out and see whether what she said would work! I saw a girl standing on her own too, and so I walked up to her and said "Hi I'm Sam, what's your name?" I went as red as a beetroot ha ha.

She seemed happy to have someone to talk to, and said her name was Chrissie. I could see that my Grandma's advice was working and so I asked another question, and then another ha ha. We decided to sit next to each other!

Guess what?

Yes, you're right! I now have a new friend! We get on really well and she lives not far from me!

Thanks so much Grandma

Grandma was very happy because she was about to see me performing in a school concert for the first time.

She came to see me before it started, took one

look at my face, saw how scared I looked and asked whatever was wrong. I told her I was feeling frightened and didn't know whether I was brave enough to go out and do my performance.

She gave me a big hug, I love my Gran's big hugs, they make me feel good! She told me it really doesn't matter if I make a mistake. She said the important thing was that I try to do it, and to do the best I could. Then she gave me a kiss on the cheek, and told me no matter what happened I would be a star in her eyes.

This made me feel good so I decided to take her advice and do the best I could.

Guess what?

I did it, and I only made one little mistake!

After the performance Grandma told me how proud she was of me.

It made me realise that even though we are scared, it is important to give things a go, and unless we do, we wont ever know whether we can succeed.

Special Note to you

The next time you're feeling scared to try something, be brave, and say to yourself "I can do this," and I bet you can!

It's such a good feeling when you find out you are braver than you think.

Grandma was right again

I
CAN
DO
IT

Chapter 5

Being Brave

I always tell my Grandma about my problems because she is easy to talk to. I am so glad she is my Gran and not someone else's.

I told her we had a school camp coming up and how my Mum couldn't go. I said I was scared to bits about going away. She told me being scared is part of growing up, that it will be fun to try new things. She said I might do things I have never done before, all my friends will be there and that I knew everyone. She said I would have lots of fun and it was a chance to give new things a go.

Then she told me something that made me think "Wow she really is clever."

Grandma said that fear is just a thought. It isn't anywhere but inside my mind. I can't touch it, it doesn't exist, and, if I didn't have a thought that brought me fear, I wouldn't be scared. She also told me that sooner or later I am going to face a fear, and she said when that happens, to say strongly to myself "I have no fear, I can do this" and then do it!

"Ooooooh but can I?"

She said it doesn't matter if I don't succeed, because I can try again, and again, until I do it.

Then she really surprised me, because she said there was success in failing. I wondered how this could be, but of course Grandma knew the answer to this! She let me know that the success is in the fact that I tried. Each time I try I will feel more confident inside.

Special Note to you

I went to the school camp and it was good fun! Gran was right, I was with my friends, so mostly I was OK with the things we did. There were teachers to look after us, and a few of the other girls didn't have their mum there either. We swam in the river, that was cool fun, and in the evening we had a fire, and were allowed to cook sausages over it. They were yummy and I ate three because they tasted so good! When I wanted to go on the flying fox I was very, very, scared. The other kids were having goes, and they were screaming with excitement, because it was such good fun. Even though I could see it was going to be fun it took me ages to be brave enough to have a go. I thought hard about what Gran said, and I knew I would feel sad if I didn't try. So I said to myself

"I am brave, I can do this."

And I did it!

It was so exciting, I loved how it made me feel. It was like I was flying through the sky. I loved it so much that I had a lot of goes. If I hadn't taken Grandma's advice I would have missed out on the most exciting part of school camp.

Hooray for Grandma she's the best

Chapter 6

Affirmations

Grandma says that positive words are called affirmations. She said they have to be spoken as though I am already how I want to be. I am quite shy and she has said that if I say "I am confident" lots of times to myself, this will help me. She told me that if I say an affirmation every day it will help me become more confident.

She thinks when I tell myself I can't do something I probably wont be able to, but when I tell myself I can, I will be able to do the things I want. She said maybe not the first time, but if I am willing to do something again, and again, until I get it right, this will change my feelings to make me more confident. I like the thought of not giving up on myself.

How about you?

Gran gave me some affirmations to use so I am sharing them with you, and I really hope you will say them too.

I believe in myself

I am happy

I am confident

I am brave

I have faith in my ability

Special Note to you

You can make up words of your own if you like, as long as they make you feel happy and strong inside. It's important to feel good about yourself don't you think? Don't forget to say them every day. I am going to say mine before I get out of bed. I will also say them any time I feel a bit afraid or unhappy, and then when I get into bed I am going to say them before I go to sleep.

Grandma has said not to stop saying them no matter how old I grow, because she said that often grown ups feel scared and not confident. She thinks that if I say them while I am growing, I will be very confident when I am a grown up! She also said that I can change the words I say whenever I want, to help me become whatever way I choose.

She said a good affirmation for me to start with would be 'I always do as I am told' ha ha

Nice try Grandma!

I
AM
FRIENDLY

Chapter 7

Making Friends

There was a new boy start in our class today. He looked shy and I thought he looked a bit scared.

I remembered how I felt on my first day and so I went over to him at break time and said hello. I also remembered that my Gran told me to ask lots of questions to someone I met for the first time, because this will put the person at ease, and help both of us with things to talk about.

I asked him lots of questions so that I could find

out about him, and it turns out that we have lots of things in common! He likes music and painting and so do I. He has an older brother and younger sister. That's not quite the same because I am older than my brother and sister.

I asked if he would like to sit next to me when we went back into class and he said he would.

After school he said thank you to me for talking to him because he had felt horrible not knowing anyone. I met his mother and she seemed very nice. She said she would arrange with my mum for me to visit his home to watch a music DVD.

Special Note to you

I am really pleased I did what my Gran suggested because I have made a new friend! It's good to know that there are other kids who get scared or aren't confident enough to talk to others isn't it?

I am glad I have my Grandma to advise me how to make myself feel better, and how to make new friends!

Thanks Grandma

There's a new family moved into our road and I saw the man who lives there carrying a boy to the car and putting him inside. Then I saw the man put a wheelchair on top of the car. This made me realise that the boy couldn't walk.

Later in the day I saw the boy at our school and realised he was going to be a new student. He was sitting in his wheelchair but no one was speaking to him. I might talk to Grandma about this because I haven't known anyone in a wheelchair before.

When I spoke to Grandma about the boy she told me he was exactly the same as any other boy except that he couldn't walk. She said he had feelings just the same as I did, and would be unhappy if nobody spoke to him. She thought he would want to make lots of friends the same as other kids do. She said I should speak to him, there was nothing wrong with his mind, only his legs!

She said I should talk to him and treat him the same as I would any other boy in school.

Special Note to you

The next day when I saw the boy I said hello to him. He told me his name was Anthony. I sat down on the wall beside his chair and he explained that he had been in an accident, and this was the cause of his not being able to walk.

I called my friends over to introduce them to him and we spent the rest of the lunchtime talking.

I am glad I took my Grandma's advice, because he really is a very nice boy, and like she says, he's no different from me or anyone else. I hope you will do the same if you ever see a boy or girl in a wheel chair.

Good advice Grandma

Chapter 8

Facing Up To The Truth

Mum had to go to work and so I stayed at Grandma's house for the day. When I walked through the door she gave me a big hug and asked what was wrong. I tried to convince her nothing was but I couldn't. Gran can always tell when I have a problem! I'm not sure how, but she only has to look at me and she can tell.

She sat me down at the table and asked me again what was wrong. I decided to tell her what had happened, because I knew she would keep asking until I gave in!

I told her I had accidentally knocked my glass of juice over on the couch and that I didn't want mum to find out. I got a towel to try and clean it up but I couldn't get all of the stain out.

Mum saw it and asked if I had done it, and I lied and said no. I knew that telling a lie was wrong, but I was too scared to tell the truth.

Grandma told me it wasn't the fact that I spilled the juice that would get me told off, it was the fact that I had told a lie. She explained that I should have told the truth and accepted the punishment, whatever it might be. She also said being honest is the best way to solve problems, and that telling lies can also hurt people in more ways than one.

Special Note to you

When my mum called to take me home I told her that I had spilled the juice and that I was sorry I lied to her. She was disappointed I hadn't told her the truth, and, as Grandma had said, it was not being honest that was worse than spilling the juice.

Mum told me I was grounded for the rest of the week, and I wouldn't get any pocket money for two weeks. She explained that my punishment wasn't for spilling the juice, because I didn't spill it on purpose, but for not telling the truth.

I know that it will be much better for me to be honest no matter what I have done. I was silly being scared of my mum, after all she loves me and wouldn't hurt me. She only ever wants to help me grow up to be a confident person. I had done something wrong, and I should have owned up to what I did straight away.

Thanks for listening Grandma

I
BELIEVE
IN
MYSELF

Chapter 9

Trying My Best

Grandma and I went to the zoo. I love going to the zoo to see the animals. When we got to the lions I told her how we had a running race coming up at school and how, for fitness, we would practice running.

I also told her how I thought I was not as fast as the other kids and that they might tease me because of this.

Grandma told me that no matter what place I came in, whether it was first or last, I will always be a winner because I had tried.

She told me I will always be her winner, and that I am her number one star! Grandma could see that I wasn't sure what she meant, so she reminded me about the time I was in a race and I came ninth out of twelve kids. I was a little upset about not moving on to the next race, but I had cheered up because she was there cheering me on

Special Note to you

I ran the race. I went as fast as I could and I came third! I was so pleased that I gave it a go. That's the fastest I have ever run in my life!

As we were lined up I said really strongly to myself "I can do this" and I felt as though I was flying through the air really fast! Not fast enough though, because I didn't win, but that didn't matter, because as Grandma has said, I did my best and that's what counts.

I love my Grandma she is so kind to me

I
AM
SPECIAL

Chapter 10

Feeling Left Out

Do you sometimes feel that you don't belong with the kids around you? Sort of left out? I know I do, and if you do then you will know how horrible it is. Sometimes I think that no one wants to be my friend, or likes me, and I am not too sure why I feel like this.

I asked Grandma how she is so clever, and she

said when she was a kid she had a lot of the same problems that I now have, and so she understands what I am going through. It made me feel a lot better knowing I'm not the only one with problems. I asked her who helped her, and she said she always asked her Grandma too.

I told her how I sometimes feel as though no one likes me, or wants to be with me. She said it's generally because at that time I'm not in a confident mood. I know this must be right, because sometimes I do feel good, and I join in with the other kids.

Grandma told me that when I am feeling in a low mood, I should change the thoughts I am having, and start telling myself I am important. She said I should smile, say how special I am, and everyone likes me. She said again, that how I feel is caused by what I am thinking. I should stop the 'Nobody wants me, or likes me' thoughts, and bring in the 'I am important, everybody likes me' thoughts.

She said she knows this isn't easy, but when I change my way of thinking, it will make me feel better about myself, and when I feel better I have to be extra brave and join in with the other kids. Grandma said this is a good way to help me become more confident.

Special Note to you

I went on a picnic with my family and other families from our Church. It was good fun, and I was feeling OK, but there was a group of kids playing cricket, and I really wanted to join in, but I didn't know them and thought they wouldn't want me anyway.

I remembered my Gran's advice, that my own thoughts were stopping me going over to them. I sat watching them, saying to myself "I am important, everyone likes me." I had to say it lots of times, and then I plucked up courage, went over to them and asked if I could play. They said yes, they could do with some help! I had good fun with them.

I was very glad I had taken Grandma's advice and changed how I was thinking. I wouldn't have had such an enjoyable time had I just sat and watched them playing.

Thanks Again Grandma

Chapter 11

Sharing

My brother had a screaming fit the other day because I wouldn't let him borrow my crayons. He went running to my Grandma. What a noise he made! Grandma managed to calm him down by giving him big hugs and letting him know what a special boy he was.

I had a feeling that calming him wasn't going to

be the end of the matter though, and I was right!

Grandma asked why my brother had been crying, although I know he had already told her. I said it was because I hadn't shared my crayons with him. She asked me why, and I let her know that earlier in the day I had asked him if I could play with his racing game, and he wouldn't let me.

My Grandma told me that everyone should share, because sharing is an act of kindness, and I should be kind whenever I can. She said that when I think about what happened, I hadn't shared with my brother because he hadn't shared with me. His behaviour had affected how I acted with him.

Special Note to you

I have thought about this, and think that when I am kind and share, other people might treat me the same way. I have to act the way I want other kids to act, and so I am going to be kind and friendly, and hope they will act the same way. Gran has said when they don't, it's them with the problem, not me.

If you are kind and friendly, and others aren't, don't change how you are, because being kind and friendly is the best way to be, don't you think?

Grandma really does know good stuff

I
ALWAYS
DO
MY
BEST

Chapter 12

I Can Do It Thoughts

Grandma explained that 'I can do it' thoughts are the same as positive thoughts, and they are more important than 'I can't do this' thoughts, which are negative.

This must be very important stuff, because she again told me that when I have a negative thought I have told myself I can't do it, and, because I have said this, I probably wont be able to.

She said that when I say I can do something

and try to do it, most of the time I will be able to. However, when I don't manage to do it first time, because I think I will be able to, I will try again, and again, until I do! She said this is what being positive is all about. Being positive is believing in myself, being confident, and when I want to be confident I have to be positive!

I wish it was as easy as it sounds, do you?

Grandma asked me which did I think would make me happy and confident. This is an easy question to answer after what we have been told don't you think? I have decided to have positive thoughts all the time!

Special Note to you

I am unhappy! I forgot about having positive thoughts today. Mrs Brown, my teacher, asked me if I would like to be in the school play. She said she thought I would be very good in it. I panicked, went red in the face, and said no! I said no because I didn't think I would be any good, even though she said I would. To be honest, I was a bit scared.

Mrs Brown didn't push me to take part and I was happy that she didn't, but afterward I was upset that I hadn't said yes because I know the other kids who are in the play will have a lot of fun.

Oh, I am so annoyed with myself, but I know now that it is my own fault for saying no, and next time I am going to do as Gran suggested, believe in myself, and say yes. By being negative, saying no, I have spoiled what I now realise would have been a positive, fun thing to do.

I can see that growing up isn't always going to go the way I want it to. I think I have to keep doing my best, and when I fail at something, I have to make sure I do better the next time. It's as Gran has said, positive thinking will make me confident.

          Thank you for the advice Grandma

I
AM
HAPPY

Chapter 13

Being Special

I am a kind kid and people like me

I stayed the night at Grandma's house, and just before I went to bed we saw a story on the TV about a boy going around from place to place doing kind deeds.

My Gran said that kindness is a special thing, that if I am kind to someone they will normally be kind back. She told me that kindness could go a long way, and that if I always try hard to be kind, this will take me further in life than being horrible.

She explained that every time I am kind, or do something for another person, it will make me feel good about myself, as well as make them feel good too. It shows that someone cares about them.

I have to remember that if I want someone to be nice to me, I have to be nice to them. She said if I'm not prepared to be nice, don't expect them to treat me in a nice way.

As Grandma kissed me on the cheek and left the room, I started to think about what she meant about kindness going a long way. I remembered about how Robert, a boy in my class, was always kind, and helped other kids with their work, and how at the end of the year he won the kindness award at our prize giving.

I think no one but Robert deserved it. He is the kindest person I have ever met, and I may never meet any one more kind in my life.

Special Note to you

I think Grandma might be right do you? It will be better to be a kind person and have lots of friends, than be a mean person and not have many. I am going to be a kind person from now on, and who knows, I may even win the kindness award this year!

Thanks again Grandma

Grandma was in the garden when we arrived for a visit. She was doing her gardening, when she called me over.

She wanted to show me a lovely flower that had grown up in between the carrots. I wondered what she was going to say, but knowing my Grandma there was going to be a reason for her pointing this out to me.

I was right! She said the flower had grown where it wasn't meant to. It had survived even though it wasn't in the right soil.

I still didn't get what she was talking about.

She said that some kids aren't happy with how they are. They may feel insecure because nothing is how they want it to be. If they can accept how they are, and decide to do their best, like the flower that blossomed in the wrong place, kids can learn and adapt to become the best they can.

Special Note to you

What a good way to look at things! I think it's helpful to know that when we don't feel too happy, or things haven't gone the way we'd hoped, when we accept that this is just how it is, and that we are still special the way we are, it will help us to be happy inside.

I like being happy inside do you?

I like that thought Grandma

Chapter 14

Feeling Important

My Grandma explained that throughout my life people might say things to me that make me unhappy. Sometimes what they say will be about me, or perhaps I might think they have said things, when they haven't. She has told me when I feel upset, I have to believe in my heart that I am special and important.

She has said there are lots of kids who feel different from other kids, and because they feel different, they think there is something wrong with them, when there isn't. She said no kid is the same as another, and it's the same with grown ups. Gran said everyone is important in their own way, and she wants me to remember this and believe it, because it's true.

She also said it's OK to be different. It doesn't mean you are bad because you are different, it makes you special in your own special way.

She told me when I have a problem it's very important to tell a grown up about it. Grown ups are there to help me, and make me feel safe.

Special Note to you

I think the most important thing my Grandma has taught me is that I can choose to be how I want. I can be strong and confident when I try hard, or I can be unhappy and have no confidence, because I don't try.

She has made me realise how important it is to be careful about the thoughts I have, and to be caring towards people, and not hurtful or cruel to anyone.

I am going to say lots of affirmations as I grow up, because I think these will help me to change into the way I want to be. I am going to try to be happy and positive whenever I can, and when I feel a bit sad, I am going to think about things that make me happy.

I am also going to be honest, because I learned by my actions that I have to be honest, because it's far worse when I'm not!

I am glad I have my Grandma to speak to when I have a problem, and I hope that when you are upset or scared you let your parents, or some other adult, know. Even when you feel you have done something wrong, it's important that you speak out and tell a grown up. Don't spend time feeling unhappy, or scared, when perhaps a grown up can help you straight away.

I hope you will also choose to be a positive, honest person, and as you grow up you are happy and have lots of friends too!

My Grandma says we are important and deserve

to be happy, strong, and confident, and my Grandma is always right! So don't ever doubt yourself, because I know you are special too!

Samantha xx

Thanks for everything Grandma

I
AM
A
CONFIDENT
KID

Kay Drummond was born in England and is now living in New Zealand.

She is married with a son and a daughter, and has been blessed with six grandchildren, four boys and two girls. Samantha is her eldest granddaughter.

Kay also has a **Self Help** website for adults www.positive-personal-growth.com and a Self Help CD The Magic Of Self Belief available on Amazon.com

Printed in Great Britain
by Amazon